I0191242

Dedication

This book is dedicated to Edna Jacks
without whose example I would
not have entertained the idea that to
stay was even possible!

Godspeed, my friend.

– Betty Lok

Published by JC Publishers
714 North Sandusky Ave
Upper Sandusky, OH 43351

STAY

Authors: Betty Lok and Lydia Miller
Copyright © 2020 Betty Lok
All Rights Reserved

No part of this book may be used or reproduced in any manner without written permission from publisher, with exception of the cover art. Every reasonable attempt has been made to identify owners of copyright. Errors or omission will be corrected in subsequent editions.

Scripture taken from the HOLY BIBLE NEW INTERNATIONAL VERSION Life Application Study Bible Copyright © 2011 by Zondervan. All Rights Reserved.

Scripture quotations also taken from The New American Standard Bible (NASB), Copyright © 1960, 1962, 1963, 1968, 1971, 1972, 1973, 1975, 1977, 1995 by The Lockman Foundation. Used by permission www.Lockman.org

BOOK DESIGNER
Brandon Mooney, Mooney Design

FRONT COVER ARTIST
Olivia Propeck
For permission with regard to artwork, contact artist at o.c.propeck7@gmail.com

STAY

Sacred Suffering
Fighting the Good Fight for Your Marriage

By Betty Lok and Lydia Miller

Introduction

GETTING STARTED   1

     God called them to stay.   1

     It takes passion to stay married.   2

     It takes strength to stay married.   2

     It may take suffering to stay married.   3

     It takes hope to stay married.   3

Chapter 1

DEALING WITH DISABILITY   5

     Foundation of Faithfulness   6

     The Choice   6

     Prayer for Strength   7

     Ask for Help   7

     God is All Sufficient - El Shaddai   8

     Practical Steps   9

Chapter 2

HOPING IN EMOTIONAL ABSENCE   11

     Physical Battles   12

     Financial Battles   13

     Health Battles   13

     Mental Battles   14

     Rehab Battles   14

     Relationship Battles   15

Victory Today   16

God is the Lord of Hosts- Jehovah-Tsebaoth   16

Practical Steps   17

Chapter 3

FINDING HELP WITH ANGER   **19**

Passed to the Children   20

Turning Point   20

The Lord is There - Jehovah-Shamah   21

Victorious Healing   22

Practical Steps   23

Chapter 4

COPING WITHOUT AFFECTION   **25**

Steps to Change   26

Slow Victory   26

Bite your Tongue   27

Spiritual Transformation   28

Looking Back   29

The Lord God Most High - Jehovah-Elyon   29

Practical Steps   30

Chapter 5

LIVING WITH PHYSICAL IMPAIRMENT   **33**

Take Care of Your Spouse   34

Build a Strong Foundation 34

Develop Common Priorities 35

I AM - Yahweh 36

Practical Steps 37

Chapter 6

WITNESSING IN UNBELIEF 39

Recognizing a Pattern 39

Returning 40

Hope Springs 41

Continued Struggles at Home 42

Miraculous, Painful Change 43

The Lord is Peace - Jehovah-Shalom 44

Practical Steps 45

Chapter 7

RESPONDING TO ADDICTION 47

Sins of the Fathers Repeated 48

Decision to Leave 48

The Dramatic Change 49

God is Conqueror - Jehovah-Nissi 50

Practical Steps 51

PARTING BLESSING 54

BIBLIOGRAPHY 60

Getting Started

Pregnant, alone, mistreated, and completely desperate – thus Genesis 16 describes the life situation of a young woman named Hagar (Genesis 16:1-13), who had been verbally and emotionally abused. As Genesis recounts, she fled from her home and found herself alone, without shelter in the desert.

Many women can relate to this young woman. It could be a sense of abandonment, having to endure neglect or abuse at the hands of someone who pledged to love them for life. Hagar, no doubt, had to ask difficult questions about where God was — did He see her, did He even care?

The answer to these tough questions for each person, as it was for Hagar, is yes, He does! Because, as with Hagar, God loves you and sees each life.

This book shares the extraordinary testimony of brave women who have revisited painful memories in the hope that their stories will offer concrete direction on staying the course in excruciating marital circumstances. Often labeled weak, unrealistic, unstable, co-dependent, and even delusional, these courageous women seek to follow God and His direction in their lives.

God called them to stay.

- They stayed because they were passionate about succeeding.
- They stayed because of a belief that God was stronger than their problems.
- They stayed when it involved suffering.
- They stayed because in God there is hope.

It takes passion to stay married.

According to Kevin Hall, author of *Aspire: Discovering Your Purpose Through the Power of Words*, "at its essence passion is sacred suffering. It's one thing to suffer and be a victim; it's an entirely different thing to be willing to suffer for a cause and become a victor."

Today, women express many acceptable reasons for leaving a marriage: "I just don't love him anymore," "My feelings of love have faded," "I just don't know what happened," or "I can't help it."

So, what does it take to overcome feelings with a choice of the will and mind? A choice to stay is not rooted in feelings. Rather, it is being called to a higher purpose, and understanding the heart of God, who will provide for that lonely, abandoned woman who feels destitute.

It takes strength to stay married.

When family, friends, counselors and today's society encourage leaving, it takes strength to stay. One woman said: "I read all the right books and went to counseling and still knew I was supposed to stay married, but did not how. At the beginning of each session with a new counselor, I told them that I was not going to get a divorce and made it clear that if that were their suggestion, I would not return. Out of all the counselors I saw over the years, only one honored my request. I knew the counselors meant well and saw the suffering I had endured, but I needed practical steps on how to stay married, of which few could offer."

That is strength. It takes a level of personal strength and determination to stay in a relationship that looks hopeless to those looking on. Isaiah 41:10 reminds us, "So do not fear, for I am with you; do not be dismayed for I am your God. I will strengthen you and help you; I will uphold you with my righteous right hand." The strength to stay doesn't come from within, from a place of personal determination. This verse says strength comes from God. He empowers each person. He provides what is needed to stay.

It may take suffering to stay married.

Sometimes suffering, and not necessarily a deliverance from suffering, is in store. While many want to believe that God wants everyone to have a comfortable, happy life. This isn't a promise. In fact, suffering often goes hand in hand with living a life for Christ. Acts 14:22 says, "Through many tribulations we must enter the kingdom of God."

Trouble is also promised in John 16:33, ". . .In this world you will have trouble, but take heart! I have overcome the world."

Most people instinctively avoid pain and suffering. The advice given to women in difficult marriages often comes from that point of view. While the avoidance of pain is natural, looking at the life of Job reminds us that suffering often has an unseen and higher purpose.

Job's friends and his wife attempted to coerce and berate him into cursing God for his unwarranted suffering. But Job chose to praise God in the midst of physical and emotional pain and rebuked his accusers. He chose to use what he suffered as a platform for pointing people to God (The book of Job).

Suffering in a painful marriage can be for that reason. It can also be for an unseen eternal glory. Paul writes in 2 Corinthians 4:17-18, "For our light and momentary troubles are achieving for us an eternal glory that far outweighs them all. So we fix our eyes on not what is seen, but on what is unseen. For what is seen is temporary, but what is unseen is eternal."

It takes hope to stay married.

Fixing an eye on eternal glory can provide needed hope. Devastating relationships can crush the spirit and make a person feel they can't go on. The feeling of heaviness from a crushed spirit takes away self-esteem, joy in life and makes the view of the future seem grey and hopeless.

The antidote to a crushed spirit is hope. Hope is strong. It is a sure, steadfast anchor. Hope has the power to provide assurance despite the waves. Psalm 42:5 points us to God: "Why are you cast down, O my soul? Why are you so disturbed within me? Put your hope in God; for I will yet praise Him, my Savior and my God." Following the call of the psalmist to put hope in God can bring an unexplained optimism.

The stories in this book will do that – bring hope through details about how these women kept their families together, helped their children succeed, marveled as their husband's hearts changed through God's power, and experienced love again. You can do it too. Look up, sweet lady. Don't give up. Choose to enter into the battle for your unique husband and marriage, your home, your family, and situation.

There is hope.

"Therefore, since we have so great a cloud of witnesses surrounding us, let us lay aside every encumbrance and the sin which so easily entangles *us,* and let us run with endurance the race that is set before us" (Hebrews 12:1).

We believe you and your story. Here are seven true stories about redemption that will amaze.

"Faith is the bird that feels the light and sings when the dawn is still dark"
Rabindranath Tagore

Chapter 1

Dealing with Disability

God is All Sufficient - El Shaddai

Things are often not what they seem. During a visit to the local radio station in town to interview the owner, it was shocking to see the man whose deep, strong voice came over the air every day. He was tall and sitting in a wheelchair-paralyzed from the neck down. His patient, relaxed conversational voice belies the body he remains trapped in, day after day.

As a young man on his way to sign up for the Navy UDT (Underwater Demolition Team), a devastating freak car accident left him a paraplegic and without a voice due to the paralysis and damage to his larynx.

To hear the kind voice directing his listeners as he comes across the radio is an inspiration. Behind that inspiring voice, is a story — not just his, but his wife's, too.

At his workstation, he has posted over the power button of his computer screen, a small white card. He shared that his beautiful wife of over 20 years had written him an encouraging poem, which she included in his lunch each day.

Foundation of Faithfulness

Although she couldn't point to the exact day when she became a follower of Christ, she was baptized at 10 years old. She testified, "I have had the instruction of obedient church attendance and felt its blessing from childhood. I lapsed while in university feeling empty that created a fissure in my relationship with God," she acknowledged. Using her degrees in administration and music, she worked as a teacher, musician, and administrator. She was filled with love, inner strength, and discernment as she lived her life to honor God.

She knew there were many decisions she made without consulting the Lord but grew to make prayer a priority. She sought peace in her life about decisions.

The Choice

One of those life changing, key decisions was to choose marriage with the radio station owner, knowing he was permanently disabled and that care giving would be part of her lifelong ministry. "I believe that part of God's purpose for my life was to enable my husband to minister over the airwaves," she explained. And it wasn't just a one-way street, for her husband brought contentment, joy, peace, and happiness to her life. "I would choose my husband as he is, over any other man on earth. God has made me love him that much."

While many people would feel put out, taken advantage of, or used, she felt called to this ministry and served with pleasure. "I am blessed and my life is wonderful," she confidently explained. Much of her selfless love was demonstrated through bearing the physical tasks her husband was unable to do. But she testified that what he lacked in physical ability, he made up for in his love for her. He encouraged her, telling her to go out with friends and not feel like a nursemaid. Though he couldn't physically do the lifting, in his wheelchair he would often roll out to the curb with her while she took out the trash and made himself available. "He often carried laundry baskets for me or kept me company when working on a project."

Prayer for Strength

Being a full-time caregiver for a quadriplegic was no easy undertaking. "Most people have no idea of the intricacies involved in taking care of a physically disabled person. My husband is almost completely dependent. If I am gone, advanced food preparation for meals is required and even planning how he will access them. A dropped meal from the refrigerator means no food until I return home."

Even helping her husband shower and dress is exhausting. During low times when she was physically tired and felt alone, she prayed for physical strength.

Her biggest concern was that as her husband aged and his health issues worsened, she might no longer be able to care for him. He regularly contracted serious lung infections and she jumped into a nursing role, helping with IV changes over lunch breaks. "Thank goodness I have always been adaptable. I sacrifice my love, time and energy for my husband. My husband is good to me."

Ask for Help

One of the toughest decisions she had to make was seeking help in ministering to her husband. He could not get up in the morning, go to bed, or prepare food by himself. When she returned home late one night and discovered he had sat unable to move from his painful position all day, the need for help became apparent.

Her feelings of guilt and fear were strong — the fear of lacking the financial means for hired help, the fear of getting a caretaker he would be uncomfortable with, and even the fear of admitting to him that she needed help were overwhelming. But she knew staying in that fearful place would create resentment and cause her to feel trapped.

Her decision was complicated by family pressure. Most of her family thought her life was too difficult given her more than two decades of the heavy physical work involved in caring for him.

The pressure of his extensive physical needs and her need for a helping hand peaked when her mother was dying. A hotel wasn't an option since, at that time, most were not wheelchair-accessible, not to mention the added expense.

While this storm of events forced her to decide to seek help, it also turned out to be a great blessing. God provided a man who came in every day to help her husband with his daily activities involved with living. The seeds of resentment that had begun to sprout in her heart were quickly weeded out. She testified, "God can turn any hardship into a blessing."

Like a breath of fresh air, the help enabled her to experience new freedoms such as being able to enjoy a weekend away with her daughters and spending more time with her grandchildren. The fear she experienced in making such a hard decision resulted in greater respect for her husband, who had always encouraged her to get help when she needed it.

God is All Sufficient - El Shaddai

The beautiful wife saw God as the all sufficient El Shaddai. Sometimes translated "God Almighty," this name of God helps to explain a part of God's character — that God is completely satisfying, and supplies strength to those who follow Him.

The lady in this story testifies: "I've often felt that I just didn't have enough faith. I thought that if I could trust God more, then things would be better. Life taught me that 'mustard seed faith' is a great blessing (Matthew 17:20)."

A mustard seed is only about 1-2 mm in diameter. Jesus said faith even that small can move a mountain! As she reflected back on her life, she saw how God had sustained her and provided the strength she needed — exactly when needed. That realization has allowed her mustard seed size faith to grow. Living and working for the Lord allowed Him to provide everything she needed.

Practical Steps

Whether marrying a disabled person was a choice, or was brought into your life through accident or injury, what patterns can be learned through this lady's example?

1. **Believe God's promises.** Romans 8:28 promises, "And we know that God causes all things to work together for good to those who love God, to those who are called according to His purpose." God will turn hard things into blessings. It starts with the decision to believe what He says in His word is true. That may sound simplistic or even unrealistic, but the mind is the beginning battleground. Don't discount setting your mind on God's promises and the truth that He can see a bigger picture than you can. Trust in that knowledge.

2. **Pray for God's help.** James 4:2 reminds, "...You do not have because you do not ask." Daily coming to God to ask for strength to provide for physical needs and emotional strength is key. Get a group of people praying for you and your husband. Find one person you can reach out to via a text message or a call who will pray with you about what is going on.

3. **Admit you need help.** Expressing this need sometimes feels like defeat. There's a great example of how God uses people to help to gain victory in life. In Exodus 17:9-13, the Israelites were in a battle. If Moses held the staff of God up high while they fought, they were victorious. When Moses' strength failed and he could not hold up the staff of God, the Israelites would begin to lose. Aaron and Hur came alongside Moses and literally held up his arms so he could hold the staff and they could win the battle. If the physical demands are too much, find a friend or caregiver to share the burden.

"If I speak in tongues of men and of angels, but have not love, I am only a resounding gong or a clanging cymbal. If I have the gift of prophecy and can fathom all mysteries and all knowledge, and if I have a faith that can move mountains, but have not love, I am nothing. If I give all I possess to the poor and surrender my body to the flames, but have not love, I gain nothing. Love is patient, love is kind. It does not envy, it does not boast, it is not proud."
1 Corinthians 13:1-4

Chapter 2

Hoping in Emotional Absence

God is the Lord of Hosts - Jehovah-Tsebaoth

Battle is an excellent word to describe the life of the veteran and his wife. They had battles in their joint service in the Air Force, battles on the home front due to his devastating health problems, which led to battles with medical professionals and against financial pressure. But most of their battles were internal and unspeakable against an invisible enemy. As Ephesians 6:12 describes, "For our struggle is not against flesh and blood, but against the rulers, against the powers, against the world forces of this darkness, against the spiritual forces of wickedness in the heavenly places."

The first time she saw him, it was far from love at first sight. "He had a real thick Boston accent, a white polo shirt, green tennis shorts, and knee-high socks with stripes that matched both his shirt and tennis shoes. I think his mom dressed him, because no one came to the base like that," she said. When he first started asking her out, she said no, and only finally agreed to a date if two friends went along. "We went to a movie. It was *American Werewolf in London*, then to Godfather's Pizza. After that he just kept showing up at my barrack's door."

His persistence paid off; she sensed he was the one and eventually said yes to his proposal. When they got married, she said, "I didn't really know a whole lot about him. I just knew to marry him was of God, and that was what I was supposed to do."

Though he wanted children right away, she held out for the completion of their military service to provide a more stable life for the children they would have. After they completed their tours, they returned to Ohio where they both got jobs at factories, which involved 12-hour changing shifts. After successful potty training of their oldest daughter relapsed due to working overtime, he told her, "… you're quitting." She did, and was home with the kids for four years.

While life started out full of anticipation, the battleground was being set in the young bride's life. She had no idea how much she would need every ounce of spiritual battle armor available to her. She would need the shield of faith, the helmet of salvation, the breastplate of righteousness, the gospel belt of truth, the shoes of peace and sword of the spirit (Eph. 6:11-18).

Physical Battles

"He came home from work one day with the flu. He shook all night so we thought maybe he had pneumonia. The next morning, I said, 'You've got to go to the hospital.'" The initial ER analysis confirmed the flu, but a follow-up doctor delivered shocking news. He said, "Your husband's kidneys are shutting down." She was told he was going to die." He was quickly airlifted to a major hospital, put on a transplant list, and she was encouraged to call in family to say good-bye.

Thankfully, that wasn't the end for him. "His siblings said they would be tested. His oldest brother was the closest match." That summer he had his first kidney transplant. It was such a good match, that the transplanted kidney would probably last the rest of his life. When, some years later, West Nile virus destroyed that kidney, she became a donor herself.

And as one battle ended, the next came. "When he lost his job, we lost our insurance. I had to go out and find a job. The first job I got was part-time. I would get up at 2 am, go to three different factories, filling their vending machines, finish by 6:30 am, get home in time to get the girls up for school and on the bus. I would do all the housework, then go coach basketball, get home and fix dinner" – a mentally and physically exhausting routine she would repeat every day.

One day at the church they attended, a 90-year-old lady asked to pray for her and said she was told by God to bring her money so she could obtain her insurance sales license. She faced this educational battle head on, took the test, 3-1/2 hours later coming out, sweating, and had to sit down. "I knew I could not afford to take it again." She passed!

Financial Battles

After his transplant, she received the first medical bill. "When I got the first bill, I called and said, 'I think you people added too many zeroes.' It was $10,000 a week. So I took money out of my 401K and paid the bill, but even with my new job it wasn't enough to cover the transplant medications."

Even their attorney said it would be best if they got divorced. "All the debt coming in- you are not responsible for it," he said. "I don't want to get divorced. I don't believe in that," she said. The attorney countered, "You know you could lose everything."

Different people at church even said, "Oh, it will be okay, you could live in the same house. It's just a piece of paper." She replied, "Well, I couldn't live with myself, if I did that." She fought this temptation, determined to stand her ground against the easy way out, despite imminent threats they would lose their home.

Eventually, declaring bankruptcy and selling their house became the only option. She struggled with feelings of failure, shame, and defeat in relinquishing the only home her children knew. She wanted to hide from the embarrassment, but she could claim God's promise, "O Lord of hosts, how blessed is the man that trusts in You!" (Psalm 84:12).

She stayed.

Health Battles

Her husband had a downturn in his health with worsening seizures and confusion, and severe signs of lethargy. Another trip to the ER resulted in a month of hospitalization, trying to find the source of his problem. Her days were again spent traveling, working, and waiting for a diagnosis. Finally, the blood work showed he had West Nile virus.

While it seemed good news that there was a diagnosis, his IVs were removed, and he was no longer quarantined, there was bad news. "The infectious disease doctor told me he would never get better. 'You will not be able to take care of him. We are permanently placing him in a nursing home to study him.'"

She knew if he came out of this, he was not going to be happy in a nursing home. Knowing their two girls still needed their dad in their lives, she turned from the temptation to sign commitment papers to release her from the burden of care he would need. Again, she could claim the Biblical truth, "...the Lord knows how to rescue the godly from trials" (2 Pet. 2:9).

She stayed.

Mental Battles

When she refused to sign those papers, professionals from the hospital appeared trying to change her mind, "You need to accept this, he is never going to be different than he is now." She said, "I was told so many times over the years he was going to die and he is still here. I really think if he is going to die, I would have a sign. He is not going to die. I don't believe that he is going to die and I think he is going to get better." The psychiatrist glancing up from her notes answered, "I think you are delusional. You are mentally unstable."

The counsel of others telling her to leave her husband was strong but she sensed an adherence to a higher authority, and the verse, "For we must all appear before the judgment seat of Christ" (2 Corinthians 5:10), made her reject the advice given on all these fronts.

She stayed.

Rehab Battles

Rather than a nursing home, her husband went from a hospital to brain injury rehabilitation. He could no longer walk. He talked like he was drunk, he wasn't all there. His Army nurse told her not to coddle him or else he would die. It seemed hopeless, but after many months of hard work and commuting for her, he defied all the odds and was headed home.

Every morning, she accepted the challenge to be his cheerleader and coach. "I would make him get up every day and I bathed him and made him walk around the barnyard. Each day he could go a little farther." Each afternoon, she left him in the care of her parents who stepped in to help when she went to work.

The battles weren't just physical. "One of the effects of West Nile virus was depression. There is nothing they can give you. It affects your brain. Doctors told me to watch him when it was gray, gloomy outside or in the wintertime. So right after Thanksgiving, I would put him on a plane and send him down to his mom's house in Florida."

As depression reared its ugly head with her husband's talk of killing himself, she removed the guns from their house. She told her husband that he needed to be around for his children. "You wanted them, so you are going to be around to help take care of them. You aren't allowed to die until I tell you, you can!"

She stayed.

Relationship Battles

Part of the struggle was that West Nile also altered her husband's personality. "When he first got back to the house after West Nile attacked his body, our daughter came home to visit. She said something and he got up off the couch and went after her, to hit her. After pushing the table between them she told her daughter, "Just go to grandma's until he calms down." He would never remember his violent outbursts and his inability to recognize how he hurt others affected their younger daughter too.

The virus also left him unaffectionate; he lost the ability to even return a hug. Shocked, her mom said at his birthday party, "Doesn't he hug you goodbye and tell you he loves you?" "No," she said, "there is nothing I can do about it. That part of his brain is never going to regenerate. Mom, I know he loves me, but it's not like Dad where he gave you a kiss every day. That's just gone."

She could have left and so many advised her to do so and ease the hardships in her life. Scripture, though, teaches, "Love always protects, always trusts, always hopes, always perseveres" (1 Corinthians 13:7).

She stayed.

Victory Today

Today the Boston lad is not in a nursing home. He and his bride are still married. The once stay-at-home mom continues to advance in the insurance industry. And her husband, "is now good. He watches our grandson who has autism. He has patience with the little guy, he really does."

She built a home that didn't fall down.

God is the Lord of Hosts- *Jehovah-Tsebaoth*

The name of God, Jehovah-Tsebaoth, which means the Lord of Hosts, is used to represent God's presence in battles as a warrior. Although many times, salvation is considered the end of spiritual battles and victory is achieved, the reality is that salvation is the date of enlistment in God's army.

As described at the beginning of this story, Jehovah-Tsebaoth is at war with the enemies of darkness. He calls Christians in 1 Peter 5:8 to "Be of sober spirit; be on alert. Your adversary the devil, prowls around like a roaring lion, seeking someone to devour." This story's strong warrior discovered strength and confidence in life came from her relationship with God. Just as she obeyed her earthly commanding officers in the Air Force, she took orders from her loving commanding officer, the Lord of Hosts. He was her ruler, her great General, King, and Commander.

She stayed in the battles of her life and stood in victory.

Practical Steps

If you are in a relationship in which your husband is emotionally absent, what can you do?

1. ***Trust* God.** While this may sound simplistic, it really is at the heart of everything. If you know God means whatever you are going through for good, your perspective changes. In Genesis 50, Joseph reflected on all of his life's circumstances, including being sold as a slave, falsely accused and imprisoned, and said in verse 20, "As for you, you meant evil against me, but God meant it for good . . . ." Trust that the living, loving God is allowing hard things in your life for a reason you may not see right now. Don't assume difficulties mean He doesn't love you or isn't with you. God has said, "...Never will I leave you, never will I forsake you" (Hebrews 13:15).

2. ***Love* and acceptance.** You may need to accept that life isn't going to be the way you envisioned and that's okay. A dream you may have had for your life may never come to fruition - for example, health and happiness. But God's ways are better, richer, fuller, even if sometimes they are harder. Love is expecting nothing in return. Love is sacrificing your wants and desires to do the will of your Creator.

3. ***Become* an advocate.** When you are in a challenging physical health battle, you need expert medical personnel and doctors who will help as you search for answers to inexplicable problems. Keep searching for answers, even if it requires changing doctors and seeking second opinions. Don't accept simple "no's." You must advocate for your spouse by writing down questions and seeking solutions. Challenge those providing for his care to keep trying.

"Love is not rude, it is not self-seeking, it is not easily angered, it keeps no record of wrongs. Love does not delight in evil but rejoices with the truth. It always protects, always trusts, always hopes, always perseveres."

1 Corinthians 13: 5-7

Chapter 3

Finding Help with Anger

God is There, Jehovah–Shamah

For nearly 20 years, a cloud of darkness remained over this home. It was a secret kept from the outside world, a hidden shame so deep it wasn't even shared in prayer circles. She sought to be obedient to what she felt scripture taught — wives were to submit to their husbands — and to the message her husband touted – there was only one king in the house and he was it. She admitted, "Most Christian writers and female speakers discuss their great marriage and wonderful husbands, I was embarrassed as that was not my truth."

It wasn't unusual for a late-night rant to begin with him flinging open the bedroom door and berating her about something she had done wrong at work or in the community he was certain caused others to not respect him. It often escalated into flying furniture, smashed pictures, and broken dishes.

He displayed a controlling spirit that was frequently accompanied by accusations, screaming, and lectures. He demanded to know where she was at all times and wanted her "home." She was required to text and phone about every move she made. Going out with friends was prohibited, which was crushing because she desperately needed the infusion of healthy relationships to build up her spirit.

Their intimate life was dutiful to her. She met his needs – despite working full-time and caring for their small children - but it was wholly without emotion and devoid of tenderness and love. There was no shared physical touch outside the act itself. He preferred not to be touched routinely. Sometimes staring at his snoring back after it was over, she felt intense disappointment, that "this just isn't fair."

Passed to the Children

Their two children also often suffered the rage he so frequently unleashed. The three-year-old would huddle behind her older brother as their father lectured them, predicting they would amount to nothing and telling them they were no good, sometimes for nearly 40 minutes. Exhausting to listen to for even two minutes, the wife would stand by helplessly, feeling powerless to intervene and stop the tirade.

At other times, she would break the church teaching about marital submission that often chained her to inaction, and run with both children to the safety of a locked bedroom. There, they would huddle together, kneeling on the floor, just breathing. Her children's pale, frightened faces assaulted her as they waited for the terror to subside and for him to leave as his anger finally abated. They felt the calm in those moments the Psalmist describes: "He will cover you with His pinions, and under His wings you may seek refuge..." (Psalm 91:4).

Turning Point

In the car one day, the thought to "just drive off the road" came into her mind. This thinking was as normal as thinking about what time she had to be at work, the children's activities that day, or what she needed from the grocery store. The consequences of that decision — that she would die and how it would affect her children — seemed suspended from her reality.

She finally saw how fractured her life was when she realized how "normal" the thought of driving her car off the road had become. So after nearly twenty years of this unending pattern, she decided to seek professional help. Her soul longed for a transformed mind and a healed life.

Sitting in the waiting room surrounded by others with clear, outward expressions of mental illness, she felt out of place. Only her black and grey clothing mirrored the hopeless despair. "I felt I didn't belong there, but I was wrong," she revealed.

The counselor told her she was suffering from severe depression, yet this was inconceivable to her, given what she knew about depression at that time. She thought a depressed person couldn't function in normal life. "I thought with depression you can't get out of bed," she relayed. Yet she began to learn about the detrimental effects of long-term stress and the chemical disruptions that happen in the brain in order to cope.

Though the diagnosis was painful to hear, hope accompanied it – hope there could be a solution. She felt the tenderness of the Psalmist's words, "The Lord is near to the brokenhearted and saves those who are crushed in spirit. Many are the afflictions of the righteous, but the Lord delivers them out of them all" (Psalm 34:18-19).

The Lord is There - Jehovah-Shamah

She sensed the presence of Jehovah-Shamah, which means the Lord is There, in her life. She began to see that her husband wasn't her primary enemy. She knew the fighting in her life wasn't just against the flesh and blood of her husband, but against Satan, who came to "steal and kill and destroy" (John 10:10).

As she looked back over the twenty painful years she had endured, she saw God had always been with her. He was there in the midst of the terror, providing a place of peace for her soul. He was her "...refuge and strength, an ever-present help in trouble" (Psalm 46:1-3).

She would remind herself each morning of the truth taped to her bathroom mirror from Philippians 4:6-8, that peace will come to those who train their thoughts to think about what is true, honorable, pure, lovely, and of good report. She began training her mind to be thankful for the smallest good she saw in her husband – protecting the family, in his own way; his hard-working attitude; and his devotion to his town, county, and nation.

Not only did she practice a change of mind, she gave herself permission to leave if she needed to.

Her emotional safety became a priority. Though he had refused counseling in the past, convinced it wouldn't work, her mind was set that counseling was imperative.

With the help of a trusted professional, they created behavioral boundaries related to the areas he struggled to control. One boundary was that if he screamed at her more than three times in a month, she would leave and stay at a hotel. He responded to the parameters set for him. She never had to leave.

She chose to stay.

Victorious Healing

Healing came slowly and steadily. Having now celebrated 30 years of marriage, they can do everyday things together, like ride in a car, eat in peace, and catch the news on television. They make funny videos on their phones to send to their professional children. They serve their community together. She saw, looking back, that Jehovah Shamah was always with her. A verse a counselor penned on an index card reminds her that, "In repentance and rest you will be saved, in quietness and trust is your strength..." (Isaiah 30:15).

Practical Steps

If you are in a relationship with an angry husband, what can you do?

1. ***Seek* professional help and counseling**. This is a great step as it gives you confidence to set practical boundaries. An objective listener, such as a good friend or pastor, can also help you decide what you could do to set protections. If you are afraid of being hurt physically, always seek help. Make a plan to leave for a safe place in the event you need it.

2. ***Read* and apply the Bible**. The word of God is an instructive manual for life, full of practical and spiritual truth. Without this knowledge, as a Christian, it's impossible to understand God's principles for how to navigate life. Learning how to study the Bible, what words mean, and HOW to correctly apply them will be transforming.

3. ***Adjust* your expectations**. While it seems the ONLY measure of healing would be for a husband to stop lashing out in anger, the truth is that life often delivers pain and suffering. The good news is that if you stay the course, trust that God has not abandoned you and accept the relationship trials as part of God's transforming process in your life, you will see results and recompense (to make amends to someone for loss or harm suffered; to compensate).

When I cannot understand my Father's leading,
And it seems to be but hard and cruel fate,
Still I hear that gentle whisper ever pleading,
God is working, God is faithful, only wait."
A.B. Simpson

Chapter 4

Coping without Affection

God is Most High - Jehovah-Elyon

"God," her husband said, "you make me miserable." The words shot through her like a knife, wounding and slashing once again. Everything in her wanted to run, to tear out of the house, slam the door and never look back. It seemed impossible to love him. She wanted to get out, to be free, to not have to endure such verbal wounds.

She stayed.

He was a successful engineer, and considered himself the head of the house. Though she was allowed to give an opinion, he always had the final say in decisions. Since he was the main breadwinner, he felt her small income from babysitting didn't make the grade, thus her thoughts did not have the same weight as his.

He seemed angry about almost everything, and the end result was usually a verbal lashing. One time after she had gotten a new short haircut, he asked why she wanted to look so hideous. They had two beautiful children and she put on some weight that didn't come off easily. "He told me he wasn't physically attracted to me anymore. That hurt a lot," she sighed.

In an attempt to keep things amiable, she often did things she wasn't comfortable with, like going to sporting events where there was drinking. She would go, cringing inside. But her compliance had little effect.

The atmosphere of combat and meanness drove her to hit back by putting him down in front of their friends. Sarcastic digs and subtle putdowns were attempts to self-soothe that never lasted. The caustic atmosphere of fighting and screaming impacted their children. The blame game was full on in the house, and neither she nor her husband were willing to change or admit guilt.

Steps to Change

Although she made daily trivial choices about what to share with friends, what to eat, where to go, and what to think about, the most pivotal choice she made was to trust Jesus Christ as her Savior. At first, the refreshing forgiveness of God washed over her soul, creating a lightness and sense of freedom she had never known before. She felt hope and promise for the future.

But soon, her newfound faith started to be a club she would wield, pointing out scripture verses in an attempt to magnify his wrongs. When that didn't work, she would go back to God and at night, lay her hands on her husband to pray. Once he jumped out of bed during her attempt to pray for him like he'd been jabbed with a pin, and yelled, "Don't do that again . . . stop it!"

She tried to be the voice of reason, wanting the conviction of the Holy Spirit to flow through her and impact him. She attempted to use her own will to change him since he was so obviously in the wrong.

One day, at the end of her rope, with all her good ideas expended, she said, "God, love him for me. I can't." In that moment of weakness, she understood it wasn't her job to tell him what to do or to change him. She finally saw the futility of trying to get him to listen. Her husband had to answer to God for his actions. She opened her hands and lifted him to God for His work.

Slow Victory

For this couple, a bolt of lightning or a group intervention didn't change their relationship. Rather, it improved day-by-day, inch-by-inch.

Just like parents instruct little children to mind their manners, she began with simple responses, saying "please" and "thank you "when he did things. Though it was hard to express thankfulness when so many other things he did were hateful and mean, she remained determined to speak kindness and love into existence. If he took out the trash, changed the oil in the car, or mowed the lawn, she expressed appreciation. If she needed something, she peppered the request with "please" and "thank you." "I asked God to open my husband's eyes to see me. I asked God to help me see my husband through His eyes. I asked God to decrease my selfishness. I asked God to help me with loneliness because I missed him so much when he was gone for work."

She knew Romans 5:8, which says "But God demonstrates His own love toward us, in that while we were yet sinners, Christ died for us." Although her husband was clearly sinning in her eyes, she knew her own sin and shortcomings, and that that God didn't judge him more harshly. She was grateful for grace in her own life.

She decided to own up to her own sin, asking her husband to forgive her for belittling him in front of his friends. She chose to stop putting her husband down, and to stop gossiping when she realized her cutting words were as Proverbs 14:1 explains that, "The wise woman builds her house, but the foolish tear it down with her own hands."

Bite your Tongue

She also recognized that she had a faith problem. "I used to pray for him to change his attitude and that he would be nicer. I prayed for my husband even though I was not happy with him. But I realized I was doing God and my husband a disservice when I did not believe God could change him," she stated.

She made the decision to use respect and to make requests instead of barking out orders. A simple shift from "You need to take the garbage out" to "Could you please take the garbage out?" positively impacted his responses.

A practical tactic she sometimes used was to literally bite her tongue! "I even had a sore jaw sometimes," she recalled smiling. Clamping her teeth down so hard that she tasted a bit of blood became a signal to go out to the garden and talk to God. Her aching jaw reminded her that God was in control. She began to live Proverbs 18:21 that teaches "Death and life are in the power of the tongue, and those who love it will eat its fruit."

God became the one she ran to with her pain and loneliness. He became her good and loving Father, husband, and friend. When she received a bitter word from her husband, she could go to the gentle One who saw her soul, who knew the retaliating snide remarks that wanted to spill from her own mouth, and would bring scripture to her that would wash away her curses. Ephesians 5:26 teaches that the word of God is cleansing and sanctifies (sets one apart), "So that He might sanctify her, having cleansed her by the washing of water with the word."

Sometimes, getting rest made a difference. When the relationship delivered mental pain rather than kindness, she found ways to refresh her body and soul. A good night of sleep, a warm bubble bath, or spending time in the back yard garden would provide a soothing respite.

Spiritual Transformation

One day, a simple miracle happened. Her husband went to church. He always bitterly said Christians were a bunch of hypocrites. He even conducted his own test during one service when the Pastor asked everyone to close their eyes and raise their hands if they wanted to be saved. He raised his hand and later told her he'd done so only to see if anyone would tell her that he had responded. No one did.

He gradually began to see Christianity in a different light. He began to change. He saw Christians as genuine and, though not perfect, real. He saw Christ lived out in her responses and change of language and tone.

One day, their daughters looked out the window and noticed he was doing yard work without his usual attitude, often expressed by throwing things and acting put out. Their daughters knew something had changed. She started seeing little things too, like thanking her for dinner and asking how he could help.

Looking Back

After years of the slow and steady daily forgiveness and reaching forward in hope, she said "Today we enjoy watching TV with one another. We are so blessed with our family and even a car that we both love to ride in. I show love by simple things, like closing the dishwasher door." They have a regular habit of saying "please" and "thank you," and practicing common courtesy and showing support of one another. They talk of the future. "We even talked about how on our deathbed we want to be together."

The Lord God Most High - Jehovah-Elyon

Jehovah-Elyon means God Most High. He is the supreme owner of heaven and earth and all people. He does the work of change and reconciliation. God delivered this family from fighting and anger when they were submissive to Him, for "...blessed be God Most High, who delivered your enemies into your hand" (Genesis 14:20).

Practical Steps

1. ***Faith* in Jesus.** The beginning of every Christian life is simply *the beginning*. Romans 3:10 tells us that there is "none righteous, no not one," and Romans 3:23 reminds us that every single person falls short of God's standard, for "all have sinned and fall short of the glory of God." The way to come into relationship with God is to ..."confess with your mouth Jesus as Lord, and believe in your heart that God raised Him from the dead, you will be saved" (Romans 10:9-10). The faith you place in what Jesus did is the *beginning* of your walk as a Christian, of a true life with Christ. Church attendance, reading your Bible, and other "religious" acts don't save anyone. They are the outflow of that relationship, but don't produce salvation.

2. ***Grace* for slow change.** While lightning-bolt change sounds preferable, usually change is a steady pace of growth. It requires lots of patience. In a strong Bible- and God-believing church, you can find strength for the daily battle and other people who can pray with and for you, and keep reminding you of God's promises that "...He is my strength and my song, and He has become my salvation..."(Exodus 15:2).

3. ***Be* slow to anger and bite your tongue.** James 3 tells us that the tongue is small but exceedingly powerful. Just as a small rudder controls a ship, or a bridle controls a powerful horse, the tongue makes big impacts. Often the best action is to keep quiet. If too many words spill out, the decision to control and lead then comes from you and it's not the work of God. Transfer your need to say things to your husband, in an attempt to change him, to God in prayer. Wait for the Lord to work.

St. Therese of Lisieux authored *The Little Way*. She described the little way as commitment to tasks and to the people we meet in our everyday lives. She believed you manifest your love for God and for others by simple, direct faith.

"Live out days in confidence in God's love for you. Recognize each day as a gift in which your life can make a difference by the way you choose to live it. Choose life, not the darkness of pettiness or greed. To offer oneself as a victim to Divine Love is not to offer one to sweetness, to consolation, but to every anguish, every bitterness, for love lives only by sacrifice; the more a soul wills to be surrendered to love the more must she be surrendered to suffering. "

Chapter 5

Living with Physical Impairment

God is Self Existent - Yahweh

A strong, muscular building contractor became disabled to the point that he couldn't even stand on his own. He had been reduced to crutches with a large base, a waddling gait, and very little lower extremity strength. His wife, an elected fiscal officer, was strong and confident. They had been married 42 years, raised three children, and she had survived four different types of cancer. And now they lived with his painful, life-altering disability. Walking on sand-covered beaches and hot tub getaways were no longer a part of their lives.

"I grew up in a family that didn't demonstrate patience or mutual encouragement. I decided long ago that I wanted a different life." She worked to break the negative cycle in which she had been entrenched. 1 Peter 4:1-2 brings the reminder, "Therefore, since Christ suffered in the flesh, arm yourselves also with the same purpose, because he who has suffered in the flesh has ceased from sin, so as to live the rest of the time in the flesh ... for the will of God." How she lived her life for the will of God was evident in all her actions.

She showed preferential concern for her husband, asking him when he wanted to stand to leave and even how he wanted to exit a room. With his limited physical abilities, it would have been easy for her to view him in a childlike manner, and direct his activities, telling him what to do and how to do it. But she didn't refer to him as disabled, for his sharp mind lived on, just in a body that had betrayed him; nor was there a hint of bitterness at the sacrifices she made.

Take Care of Your Spouse

One simple practice she had engaged in for years was having a hot meal ready when he got home from work. While many working women with full-time jobs may feel it's not their duty to cook when they are also putting in many hours a day, this confident woman was not bound by obligation, but chose to serve her husband in this way. "I fed him so he could work and I would have supper ready for him before I left for work. I took care of him so he could excel at his job."

It was an expression of her love and appreciation for all he did, as well as a way to encourage her husband to succeed. Feeling appreciated motivated him to work hard and excel. She felt truly grateful for him and practiced the Proverbs 31:12 example of an excellent wife who "...does him good and not evil all the days of her life."

Build a Strong Foundation

This strong marriage wasn't built on sand (Matthew 7:26-27). They had a solid foundation, the bedrock for their relationship. They agreed upon and committed to three strong building blocks that were essential for their success as a couple:

1. A foundation was their intimate relationship. They became keenly aware that they each approached this area differently. For the husband, expressing physical love to his wife WAS true love. She felt, "If a woman feels loved emotionally with kind words or gifts or acknowledgment she is more likely to want to have sex". As they learned about their differences, they could appreciate the expressions offered and understand the motives.

2. Another foundation block was money. They shared the principle that they wouldn't just work for a paycheck. The paycheck was just a springboard, a tool to be used to build their lives. They agreed on a spending plan and made sure they could both use their financial resources in ways that made them happy. Planning for the future financially and in other ways brought them peace of mind.

3. The third area was trust. They were honest and truthful with each other. They always looked at their marriage as a team operation. She believed, "Vows are vows and I feel that marriage is not disposable." They both had separate interests in projects and she often encouraged him to do things that interested him, making him feel important, appreciated and needed. He was different physically, which is all many people would see, but she knew the real man underneath and that's the man she focused on. A further part of working on trust involved her having healthy female friendships just for fun and sharing life with.

As husband and wife, they trusted each other for the decisions and choices they made, ensuring there was no opportunity to play the blame game for outcomes they didn't like. They made the decision early on to forgive, and to not respond in a mean spirit or hold grudges.

While hot-tubbing was not possible given his disability, they sometimes symbolically sat *beside* the hot tub, holding hands, sharing life, and expressing gratitude for all they *did* have. "Just getting through the day and knowing we did it together was enough."

Develop Common Priorities

In addition to the foundations of meeting each other's physical needs, sharing financial goals, and developing trust, their family, children, and home were also essential building blocks in their lives.

Work was a tool that allowed them to build a home and love their children and family. As an elected fiscal officer, when someone would seek her out to network, she was hurt when they often turned away when realizing the depth of her commitment to keep her home and family a priority. "I would let it go by doing something productive and not dwelling on it."

She recognized that her marriage was a gift. She held her vows reverently and with great strength. She found the best way to build a strong home was to deal with issues as they arose, accept her husband as he was and always hold the lines of communication open.

I AM - *Yahweh*

One of God's great names is Yahweh. It was such a sacred, holy name that Jews in the Old Testament left the vowels out and wouldn't even pronounce it. You could boil a definition down to the words "to be." Jesus declared He always was, letting everyone know He was God. Knowing He is God gives strength to people struggling in difficult physical circumstances. Deuteronomy 31:6 says, "Be strong and courageous, do not be afraid or tremble at them, for the LORD (Yahweh) your God, is the one who goes with you. He will not fail you or forsake you."

God's presence allowed this gentle woman to be strong, respectful, and kind to her husband. The presence of Yahweh in the past, present, and future brings confidence that enables His children to live a life that honors God. He is the self-existent One that has always been. Yahweh saw her broken childhood relationships and He provided all she needed to break the cycle and live a courageous life.

Practical Steps

If you are living with a spouse with physical impairment, what can you do?

1. **Show Respect.** While it might be easy to jump into the director's chair in a relationship with a spouse that is limited physically, the principle of showing respect will always bring positive results. Ephesians 5:33 teaches wives to, "...see to it that she respects her husband." This basic display of deference can help a man feel internal strength to go on when dealing with tough physical restraints.

2. **Communicate.** Talking through difficult situations is essential. Decide in calm times how to deal with unusual things that may be unique to your relationship. Staying on the "same page" about money, intimacy, and how to deal with struggles builds trust that will increase happiness and joy.

3. **Change Your Attitude.** Pastor Charles Swindoll said, "The longer I live, the more I realize the impact of attitude on life. I am convinced that life is 10% what happens to me and 90%, how I react to it." If you are dealing with physical impairment in your marriage, sometimes the only thing you can change is how you respond to the situation. But your very response will change how you feel.

"But everyone who hears these words of mine and does not put them into practice is like a foolish man who built his house on sand. The rain came down, the streams rose, and the winds blew and beat against that house, and it fell with a great crash."

Matthew 7:26-28

Chapter 6

Witnessing in Unbelief

God is Peace - Jehovah-Shalom

W hen a divorcee with two young sons, who had long felt hopelessness and emptiness, met the gorgeous, strong, man, it was as if a fresh breeze blew over her life, bringing hope and promise. Her love was intense and he returned her love. "I worshipped him," the young bride remembered. They dated for seven wonderful months and then married.

Things were so exciting and enjoyable — for two weeks. The first payday, things quickly turned. He didn't come home after work that night and when he did, he was drunk. She soon learned he had kept this addiction hidden from her in their months of dating. Not only was he drunk, that night he became violent, revealing the first signs of his alter ego. The next morning, though he knew he had lashed out at her and felt shame, he couldn't recall the details.

Recognizing a Pattern

This pattern of these first two weeks would repeat over and over as the years went on. He became resentful of her two children from a previous marriage, and was even jealous of her expressions of love to them. If he came in when they were laughing, he would yell, "What the h—l is going on in here?", effectively shutting down the least bit of fun and negatively impacting his relationship with the children.

His possessive spirit extended toward her family and friends; he did not want her to have other relationships. He kept her beaten down with faultfinding, sarcasm, and rude comments. She always walked on eggshells since he was unpredictable and unreasonable. "He was demanding and tired all the time" she said, which eliminated normal life for her and the children.

As the situation became progressively worse, she made the excruciating decision to leave with her children. While this seemed like the only option at the time, soon after leaving she discovered the happy news that she was pregnant. "I broke with him three months after we were married but went back when I found out I was pregnant. I was not going to raise his child by myself," she resolutely explained. She knew working and providing for her children alone would be too much. And in spite of his painful treatment, realizing she was carrying *his* child overwhelmed her. She knew he longed for children of his own, so she made the difficult choice to go back - to stay.

Returning

Returning with the anticipation of a shared new life between them did make a difference. He made some significant changes in how he treated her. But the precious new baby wasn't long for this life, dying three days after birth. It was a crushing and sorrowful time. Hope renewed when she learned the happy news she was pregnant again. But this time, she only carried the baby for six months, went into labor, and suffered more sorrow when he died two hours later. Another funeral.

They were eventually blessed with a healthy son and daughter. But that wasn't enough to bring lasting change. During all these years, the alcoholic continued drinking, accusing, threatening, and even talking suicide. "I was defensive and not treated like a human being," she bravely recalled. He and his side of the family did not get along, and their disagreements often preceded heavier drinking and mental and verbal abuse toward his wife and the children.

Her life was like a ping-pong match, back and forth, repeating the same cycles. "I walked on eggshells," she explained. She would try hard to please him, but it was virtually impossible. He would brag about other women in his life and put her down in front of others. "When he would go to work, I would pray that he would have a wreck and die on the way home," she confessed.

Her mind was weary, her heart crushed. She hated her life. At times her sorrow was so intense that she wanted to escape in death herself. One dark day, she leaned against the kitchen wall and said, "Is this all there is to life? I wish I could die."

But as she heard the happy sounds of her children playing on the floor at her feet, she knew ending her life wasn't an option, for her love for her children was too great.

Although she didn't know it then, God saw all her tears. Psalm 56:8 says "...Put my tears in Your bottle. Are they not in Your book?"

Hope Springs

Three days after that moment in the kitchen when she asked, "Is this all there is to life?" a woman came to her door from a local church. She talked with her and began to tell her about Jesus and His love. She returned with three ladies who led her through the book of Acts. She said, "I really didn't want to hear it." As they left, they challenged her to read all of Acts and promised they'd be back the following week.

They called the next week to reschedule, bringing great relief to the gal who didn't want anything to do with religion. She didn't want to read the Bible and didn't care what it said. As the next meeting date loomed, she succumbed to pressure and read through Acts as fast as she could so she could say, "There, at least I did it."

After closing the book, she went to do the dishes and felt a strong hand on her left shoulder. At first, she thought it was her husband. But then she heard a prompting. He called her by name and said, "Go read it again."

Moved by this direct, deeply felt message, she once again found her spot at the kitchen table and started to read. This time, the thoughts and feelings were vastly different. She began to feel an opening in her soul and spirit. The message of the book felt as if it jumped off the page and into her heart. She was overwhelmed and tears began to run down her face, "Why didn't anyone ever tell me this?"

She felt the Lord's presence in that kitchen, surrounded by dishes and all the stuff of life. Suddenly none of it mattered. She felt the sweet presence of a loving Father. In that moment, she realized Jesus knew the hurt, bitterness, and resentment she felt about the wounds of her life and from her husband. As she surrendered her hurt and pain, something wonderful happened. "I went to the Lord and asked for forgiveness in the name of Jesus," she said smiling. She came face to face with the Lord Jesus Christ and accepted His free gift of salvation. It was life transforming – as if her story could be one of the miracles she had read about in the book of Acts.

Continued Struggles at Home

Things at home didn't change in the same miraculous way as her spiritual awakening had occurred. "I wasn't allowed to talk on the phone, and he wouldn't let me go to church," she said. She found pastors and programs she could watch and listen to and God found a way to bring church to her. Eventually her husband relented, allowing her and the children to attend church on Wednesdays, with strict instructions to come straight home. With the growth of her faith, when things would get unbearable, she would go to Jesus. He was always there to encourage her and He brought people into her life who helped carry her load of pain and struggle.

One day, her intoxicated husband was again talking suicide. She sought wise counsel from her Pastor about what to do. The words he shared would stay with her through many years to come. He said, "The Spirit of the Lord is telling me that you may be the only link to salvation that your husband will ever have." It was not easy, but she had the inner strength of the Holy Spirit who was always with her.

She stayed.

Miraculous, Painful Change

In the later years of his life, her husband was diagnosed with Polymyalgia Rheumatica (PA), a rare form of arthritis that affected his leg muscles. He also was diabetic and had neuropathy in his feet. He had to endure many different surgeries to deal with blood clots and pain. He had been a machinist but had to take early retirement when the illnesses progressed.

During his 80th year, his health began a rapid decline as PA took control of his whole body. He knew he was dying. Her own body felt near collapse from exhaustion. "For months, I would pray for God's perfect will and way to be done throughout the day in my life and my husband's." She asked for His wisdom, guidance, direction, strength, and His patience to do what she needed to. She was in a continual state of prayer. Day by day those prayers were answered.

She was able to put herself in her husband's place and recognized how she would want to be treated if she were ill, despite the life he had lived and the treatment he had doled out. She had a gifting of the Holy Spirit to show the fruit of kindness and love, to have internal peace, and to show patience and gentleness. She became an instrument — the hands and feet of Jesus to her husband. He didn't deserve it and it wasn't in her to give.

She became more compassionate, which was essential as she assumed the role of home caregiver. She literally took care of him and she saw a change in his attitude. "I knew that we are to treat others as we would like to be treated. I knew that if it were me I would want people to be compassionate, understanding, not angry, spiteful or uncaring," she said. I prayed that Jesus would let His compassion flow through me and He did. That is how I made it through all those months and years of his illness. Jesus knew how much we both could take and how beaten down physically, mentally, and emotionally I was and God took over," she explained.

Her husband physically needed her and expressed that. About three months before he died, he screamed out, "I'm sorry! I'm sorry for the way I treated you! Will you forgive me?" Thankfully she was able to say, "I forgave you a long time ago." She kneeled down at his rocker, "More than anything, I want you to know you are saved before you leave this earth."

Just a few days later, he was taken to the hospital. A pastor friend of hers visited him and shared the good news about Jesus and the plan of salvation. Her husband accepted the free gift of eternal life that day as Romans 6:23 describes, "For the wages of sin is death but the free gift of God is eternal life in Christ Jesus our Lord." Nine days later her husband died.

Isaiah 61:1 reminds people that Jesus was sent to "bind up the brokenhearted." The wife experienced heart and mind healing and testifies that Jesus can produce this for others too. She prayed one day after her husband died, "Lord, if the only reason you brought us together was to lead us to You, it was well worth it."

"No matter what anyone else does it is not worth losing your soul over what they are doing. Pray for them and put them in God's hands," she expressed.

The Lord is Peace - Jehovah-Shalom

The name of God, Jehovah-Shalom, means whole, finished, fulfilled, perfected; the harmony and reconciliation of a relationship made possible by the payment of a debt. Her peace was determined by her sanctification and trust in her Savior, Jesus Christ, not by a change in her circumstances. Isaiah 26:3 promises "The steadfast of mind You will keep in perfect peace, because he trusts in You."

This daughter of King Jesus learned that the path to peace and freedom wasn't circumstantial. It was through a fixed mind. This woman's pain and suffering weren't her only considerations. She had to make a choice of her own free will, laying down her hopes and desires for her husband. She had to "suffer according to the will of God . . . entrust their soul to a faithful Creator in doing what is right" (1 Peter 4:19).

In this obedience, she felt peace and freedom. The Lord became her peace.

Practical Steps

If you are in a relationship with an unbelieving spouse, what can you do?

1. **Be hopeful.** We serve a God who is in the changing people business. Jeremiah 29:11 says "For I know the plans I have for you, declares the Lord, plans for welfare and not for calamity, to give you a future and a hope." Fixing your eyes on Jesus and having faith in what you cannot see right now can make a huge difference in how you go through your struggles. Don't underestimate the value and power of hope. It is not God's will that any should perish without knowing Him (Matthew 18:14); trust that He is fighting for your husband.

2. **Be compassionate.** It's especially tough to be kind to someone who has been mean to you for so long, but showing kindness and compassion may very well be a tool God will use. Trust that the fruit of the Spirit of God – love, joy, peace, patience, kindness, goodness, faithfulness, gentleness, and self-control – can come through you as you surrender to Him (Galatians 5:22-23). Remember that the kindness of God leads us to repentance (Romans 2:4). You can show kindness and compassion when you see your husband as a human being made in the image of God, thus a sacred being worthy of respect.

3. **Find ways to meet spiritual needs.** When an unbelieving spouse refuses to let you go to church or discourages you from fellowship, you'll need to get creative in connecting with other believers and getting spiritual food for your soul. Some creative ways are seeking strong teaching through a television preacher, an online broadcast, or a Christian radio station. Other great resources could be a private internet group you can connect with, or reading Christian authors who write about topics that would encourage you.

"So God created mankind in His own image, in the image of God He created them; male and female He created them." Genesis 1:27

Chapter 7

Responding to Addiction

God is Conqueror - Jehovah-Nissi

A Halloween night blind date and a last-minute cancellation brought a 22-year-old member of the United States Air Force and Native American of the Crow Nation, and a sweet 18-year-old girl together. Though they hit it off right away, he wanted her to know up front that his heritage as an American Indian was a crucial part of his identity.

Having grown up in Montana on a reservation, he was very strong willed. One side of his personality and determination came from a large family of seven siblings and enduring an abusive stepfather who took him to church on Sunday and beat him during the week. Characteristic punishment for wrongs would be kneeling on a broomstick for hours. Though he was proud of his heritage, his experiences growing up were not healthy and contributed to his later downward spiral.

The young Ohio gal grew up with a father who was a World War II veteran, having served as a staff sergeant and a tank driver of the H Company of the 33rd Armored Regiment. Her home was a calm one that reflected her father's orderliness and military approach to the family. She was never yelled at or hit. "I didn't care that he was a Native American. He was my first boyfriend. I fell in love," she fondly recalled. They eventually married and moved to Montana.

Sins of the Fathers Repeated

After returning from his service in Vietnam, he began to have trouble with anger and self-control and often turned to alcohol to cope. He seemed a changed man from the one she married. One night when he was soundly sleeping in bed, she touched his toe to wake him. "I ended up on the other side of the room and learned the lesson of not touching him without announcing it first," she said.

The next seven years included 14 moves from Montana to California. For her husband, this was a completely normal experience as he had moved on and off reservations frequently throughout his childhood. Unfortunately, being drunk and lashing out in anger became regular practices of his as well.

Often, she was so mentally exhausted that each morning she cried out to God for a renewed spirit, "If you want me to keep on, you will have to give me the strength." Every day she did feel an infusion of God's power. She also needed help with her own feelings, for she knew she no longer loved her husband. The words of 2 Corinthians 12:9 rang true: "...My grace is sufficient for you, for power is perfected in weakness...".

She stayed.

Decision to Leave

After six years of the cycle of abuse, drinking, verbal, and sometimes physical abuse, she made the excruciating decision to leave. She went back to Ohio with their children to live with her parents.

Three months after arriving in Ohio, her son started getting inexplicable nosebleeds. The doctor felt he had leukemia. She felt compelled to let her husband know and he hitchhiked from Montana to Ohio. Soon after his return to the family, their son's nosebleeds stopped and his health returned. The children began to show signs of happiness with the family reunited.

The Dramatic Change

Back together again in Ohio, the same marriage struggles remained and many of the old feelings of fear again surfaced in her heart. After some time at the new job he had found, a co-worker invited him to church. A miraculous change occurred in his life as he saw his sin for the first time. He heard the message in Romans 3:23 that "All have sinned and fall short of the glory of God." He recognized how "God demonstrated His love toward him" when he was still a sinner (Romans 5:8). At that simple church service, he accepted the Lord Jesus as his personal Savior.

His change was immediate and dramatic. He quit drinking and God began to make the "old things pass away . . . and all things become new" (2 Corinthians 5:17). She knew he was sincere when she saw his first real smile. The change wasn't just on the surface, but down deep in his heart and it radiated out into his face and his demeanor. He went on to overcome the crippling childhood message that he was worthless and wouldn't amount to anything by getting his degree in engineering.

At the same time, their relationship underwent a dramatic transformation. They attended church together and sought to raise their family in the nurture and admonition of the Lord. The past hurts of his childhood no longer seemed to have power over him and he truly became a man "after God's own heart" (Acts 13:22b). They learned to wield spiritual weapons against the devil (Ephesians 6:10-18) when he wanted to author arguments and produce fear between them. They rebuked this enemy and felt peace restored to their relationship.

The transformation in their marriage eventually led them to full-time ministry, traveling all around the state of Ohio to share their testimony of how a relationship with the living, loving God made all the difference. Their message included challenges to young couples considering marriage to be friends first and to know Jesus Christ as a personal Savior before committing to marriage. They believed their spiritual connection was the foundation to their success.

Today, their children testify that their parents are joined "at the hip" and inseparable. "My husband is my best friend. I love traveling and spending time with him." And when he, an adopted child of God, reflects on his troubled childhood, he praises God that he is the sole sibling of the eight in his Crow Indian family who is still married.

God is Conqueror - *Jehovah-Nissi*

God is Conqueror is the definition of God's name, Jehovah-Nissi. In the Old Testament, a victorious, conquering army would carry a banner or a flag up high to symbolize victory. It was a cloth inscribed with words of victory, a coat of arms symbol, a logo, or an announcement. This is much like how the red, white and blue American flag symbolizes the freedoms fought for in the brave early battles of this country.

Though she thought when she walked away it was the end of their marriage, she didn't feel a conquering spirit. If she had carried a marriage banner at that time, it would have been torn and bruised, reflecting the damage done during years of abuse and neglect.

She clung to God as Conqueror. He led her in victory when it no longer safe for her and her children to stay; when her son needed his father and she called him to come; and when she faced the prospect of a life as a single parent. In those moments, God was her leader, her banner. She trusted in God when she made those hard choices. She practiced Psalm 62:8 that reminds "Trust in Him at all times, Oh people, pour out your heart before Him; God is a refuge for us."

Practical Steps

If you are living with a husband struggling with addiction, what can you do?

1. ***Set Boundaries.*** There may come a point at which leaving for the bigger purpose and goal of bringing about change is necessary. Leaving when you don't feel safe is crucial. Never stay when you are concerned for your safety or your children's. Reaching out to family or a shelter is a great resource when you need it. Don't feel guilty at all; this is a part of the process some husbands need to go through. Boundaries by definition are walls of protection, just like the fence surrounding a children's playground.

2. ***Don't focus on the circumstances.*** It would be easy to set your eyes on just what you can see and feel utter discouragement. Hebrews 12:1-2 encourages that, "...we have so great a cloud of witnesses surrounding us" and we are to "run with endurance the race that is set before us, fixing our eyes on Jesus, the author and perfector of faith . . . ." You aren't alone for there is a great cloud of believers cheering you on. When you fix your eyes not on what you can see, but on what God promises, your daily joy increases.

3. ***Don't let fear control.*** When you've been in an up and down relationship for so long, it would be easy to let fear be a constant companion. The Bible is filled with challenging verses that encourage us to be strong and courageous: "For God has not given us a spirit of timidity, but of power and of love and discipline" (2 Timothy 1:7). Fear is a tactic of the enemy to keep us from victory. "Resist the devil and he will flee from you" (James 4:7).

"Yet the Lord longs to be gracious to you; therefore, He will rise up to show you compassion. For the Lord is a God of justice. Blessed are all who wait for Him."

Isaiah 30:18

Parting Blessing

Dear Beautiful, Strong, Courageous Woman,

You are the beloved of God. "He will take great delight in you; He will quiet you with His love; He will rejoice over you with singing" (Zephaniah 3:17). Our goal in sharing the stories of the seven women in this book is to give you a spirit of hope and anticipation for the future. Each of these women had a difficult path to follow, each life story was monumentally different from the others, yet they all struggled and had intense pain.

The common thread in each story was actually good news! In spite of feeling afflicted, wounded, crushed, or alone with problems, we can draw strength from the truth that God binds up broken hearts. He does not forsake believers. He brings healing.

Just like bindings in medicine keep ends of a wound together to protect it from harm and encourage healing, Jesus echoed the words of Isaiah 61:1 when He said "He (God the Father) has sent me to proclaim freedom for the prisoners and recovery of sight for the blind, to release the oppressed..." (Luke 4:18).

No one denies the oppression, pain, and difficulty that living in a hard marriage can bring. In fact, it's okay to be sad and experience grief and anger. Jesus modeled grief when He mourned over Lazarus' death, "When Jesus heard what had happened, He withdrew by boat privately to a solitary place" (Matthew 14:13), and "Jesus wept" (John 11:35).

It's possible that the struggle won't have a positive and swift healing. It may not be until heaven that complete healing will come. First Corinthians 15:58 reminds us to "be steadfast, immovable, always abounding in the work of the Lord, knowing that your toils in the Lord are not in vain." This verse reminds each person that the struggle isn't without a purpose.

While it would be enlightening to know God's purpose in the pain He allows, scripture tells us, "His thoughts are not our thoughts and His ways are not our ways" (Isaiah 55:8). Courage can come from remembering the promise, "Have I not commanded you? Be strong and courageous. Do not be afraid. Do not tremble for the Lord your God is with you wherever you go" Joshua 1:9-10.

God's purpose is seen in the book of Genesis and the story of Hagar. He called her by name, His name, El Roi, which means The God who sees (Genesis 16:13). He met her in that desert place, in her moment of greatest need and weakness. He reminded her she wasn't forgotten, that He would soothe and comfort her, and be the husband and father of her child she didn't have.

Just as God provided for Hagar, He provides for everyone who puts their faith and trust in Him (Romans 10:9-10). His provision comes to those who are too tired to even pick up the Sword (the word of God). The God of compassion and comfort is near (Psalm 147:3). Remember these encouraging truths:

❖ He is the Lord of the greatest army and He will fight *for* you. As Exodus 14:14 reminds us "The LORD will fight for you; you need only to be still."

❖ He already sees the ending of your story and He promises, "For I know the plans that I have for you, declares the Lord, plans for welfare not for calamity to give you a future and a hope" (Jeremiah 29:11).

❖ Hold on for the victory and deliverance He promises. "...Thanks be to God! He gives us the victory through our Lord Jesus Christ" (1 Corinthians 15:57).

❖ When the world tells you are weak, remember that God sees you as a strong warrior, clothed in His battle armor (Ephesians 6:10-18).

❖ When you feel He can't really know what's going on in your life, remember that He "knows your name" (John 10:3), the very number of hairs on your head (Matthew 10:30), and you are "engraved on the palms of My hands"(Isaiah 49:16).

❖ He loves you so much that He "sent His one and only son to be the Savior of the world, that whoever believes in Him will not perish but have eternal life" (John 3:16).

May God guide you and bless you

May He make His face to shine upon you.

May He offer you His blessing and give you His peace

Until we meet on earth or in Heaven someday.

Betty Lok and Lydia Miller

Note: "In researching the proper use of capitalized pronouns in reference to our Lord, we were surprised to find that this practice seems to have fallen out of favor simply because some modern Biblical translations did not use it. Various authors do not capitalize "he" and "him" when referring to God, Jesus, or the Holy Spirit to maintain consistency in literary style when quoting from these Biblical texts.

We, however, in reference to God, have chosen to use the capitalized "He" and "Him." How important is "consistency in literary style" when compared to the sacrifice Christ made on the cross? Surely our Creator, Redeemer, and Sustainer deserves the proper pronouns and much more," Michelle Burch-Morehart.

Author Bios

Betty Lok

Betty is a wife of 30 years to Kevin Lok and a mother to Catherine and John Lok. She loves being a chiropractor in Ohio and sharing her children's books.

Lydia Miller

Lydia has been happily married to Steve since college graduation. They've been blessed with five children and a growing passle of grand children.

She has served as a pastor's wife and worship leader and enjoys helping people tell their stories.

Bibliography

Lok, Betty. *The Shrewd Christian Businesswoman.* Upper Sandusky, OH: JC Publishers, 2018.

New American Standard Bible, *Life Application Study Bible,* Hardcover. Zondervan, Copyright © 1960, 1962, 1963, 1971, 1972, 1973, 1977, 1995 by the Lockman Foundation. www.Lockman.org All Rights Reserved.

NIV Life Application Study Bible, ©2011 by Zondervan. All Rights Reserved.

Sumrall, Lester. *The Names of God.* New Kensington, PA: Lester Sumrall Evangelistic Association, Whitaker House, 1982.

www.ingramcontent.com/pod-product-compliance
Lightning Source LLC
Chambersburg PA
CBHW071931020426
42331CB00010B/2822